D0095590

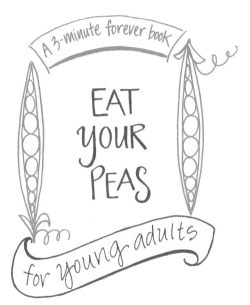

A 3-minute forever book

EAT
YOUR
PEAS

for young adults

written by Cheryl Karpen
illustrated by Sandy Fougner

Dedicated
to
Maddy

At the **heart** of this
little book
is a

# promise

It's a promise
from **me**

_____

to **you**

_____

and it goes like this...

If you ever need someone to talk to,
( cry or brag with )
someone to **hear**,
(really hear)
what's **on your mind** and **in your heart**...

# Call me.

Call me early. Call me late.

Just... call me!

And I **promise** to listen to you
with all my heart,
with all my attention,
and without interrupting.

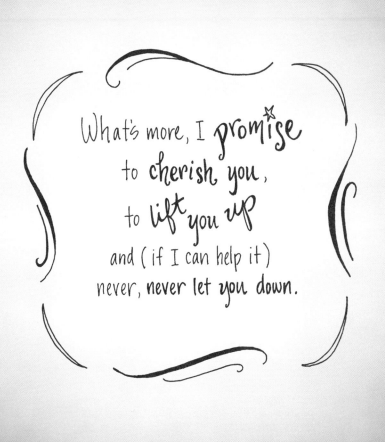

What's more, I promise
to cherish you,
to lift you up
and (if I can help it)
never, never let you down.

_____

My name
( just in case you forgot who cares about you )

_____

and my phone #.

Meanwhile, here is my
absolutely no-strings attached FREE ADVICE
for getting the most out of your
✻ amazing life! ✻
So give a listen because this is your

mom, dad, aunt, uncle, sister, brother,
grandma, grandpa, neighbor, friend, boss, teacher,
or other interested person who cares enough
to give you this hugely

straight-from-the-heart

little book.

Here goes!

Believe
in
yourself.

I do.

You
are
* enough. *

You are pretty or handsome enough.
You are smart enough.
You are worthy enough.

You are enough just the way you are!

# Be kind.

Be really *kind and gentle* with yourself.

When you
**compare**
yourself to others
it will probably make you
*un*happy.

And that's the truth.
**The real truth.**

Yes, you are *different*.

psst... we all are
and we're **supposed** to be!

# Keep a gratitude journal.

**You'll be amazed**
at what it will do for you on those days
when you are *absolutely convinced*
*you'll never be happy again*

and your life

is going down the tubes and your
boyfriend or girlfriend just broke up with you
and you're utterly miserable
**and you need something**
**to give you HOPE.**

*( psst... always hold on to hope )*

Never, ever
be afraid to say
the words

"I need help."

Whisper them. Or shout them.
But by all means get them out.

We all have
CHOICES.

Treat them with the
RESPECT
you deserve.

Surround
yourself
with
Positive people.

Keep setting new goals.
Like a good warm-up,
they make you
stretch
and keep you
limber
for the long run.

TRUST
in
a
Higher Power.
Your joy in life
depends on it.

It's okay to

ASK.

Why not *give* others
the **opportunity** to help *you*?

$S$ometimes **not** getting
what you want
is the
very best thing
that could happen to you.

( **BIG** piece of advice coming up next. )

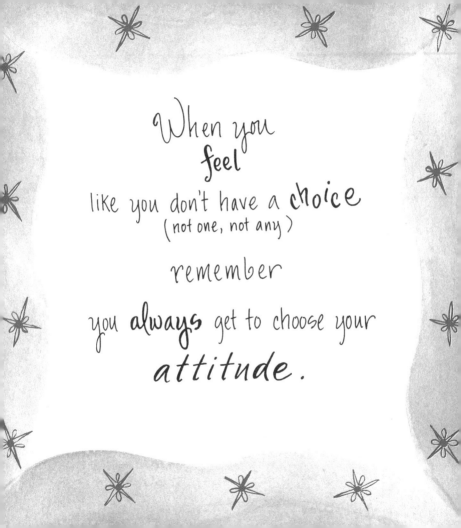

When you
**feel**
like you don't have a **choice**
( not one, not any )

remember

you **always** get to choose your
*attitude*.

When
you
practice

forgiveness

life will be much

yummier!

Before you *jump*
to **conclusions** about another
amazing (temporarily annoying)
human being,

put yourself in their shoes.

It may not be a perfect fit,
but you'll never forget the *feeling*.

Nothing
is
harder to resist
than
a
smile.

Ask any mirror.
(what works for mirrors, works on people too.)

Accept change.
It's
full of
surprises
you won't want to miss.

Almost end of free advice.

# You are a very important somebody.

No matter where you have come from,
no matter what experiences you have had,
no matter how crazy or sane
you *think* your family is,
no matter how large or small
the house you live in is...

You are a very important somebody.

## No one can take away your magnificence!

You are an **amazing person**
with a lifetime of *exciting* possibilities
ahead of you.

Have **fun!**
(Take care of yourself.)

***Go*** places!
(Take care of yourself.)

**Do** things!
(You guessed it...
Take care of yourself.)

and remember to always...

*eat your peas!*

A
very special
**thank you** to...
creative editor, Suzanne Foust
for her **spirited** play with **words**
and to
artist extraordinaire, Sandy Fougner
who ate, slept, and lived with
∘° ∘ **peas in her head** ∘ ∘°
during the **creation** of this little book.

Three peas in a pod!

Suzanne  Cheryl  Sandy

Other gift books by Cheryl Karpen

To Let You Know I Care

Can We Try Again?
finding a way back to love

Hope for a Hurting Heart
a little book of hope and self-care

For more information contact:

Gently Spoken Communications
PO Box 245
Anoka, Mn 55303
1-877-224-7886

www.gentlyspoken.com